My Berlin

Oma's
Secret Recipe

ALSO BY CHRISTEL ALEXANDER

My Berlin: Childhood Reflections
(Print Edition)

My Berlin: Childhood Reflections
(Audio Book)

My Berlin: Reverberations
(Songbook)

My Berlin: Reverberations
(Music CD)

For more information contact:
info@ckamusic.com

My Berlin

Oma's
Secret Recipe

by

Christel Alexander

CKA Music

A CKA MUSIC BOOK

TEXT

SONGS

Published by CKA Music
2801 Ocean Park Blvd, Suite 395
Santa Monica, California 90405
info@ckamusic.com

ISBN 978-1-941048-00-9

First Edition

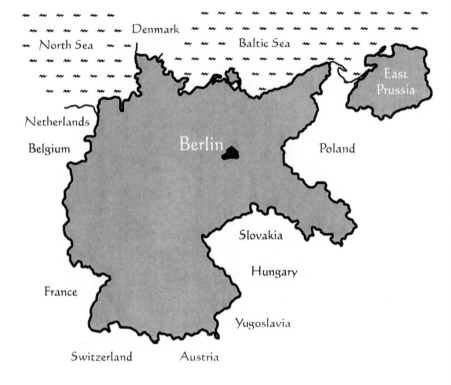

Denmark

North Sea

Baltic Sea

East Prussia

Netherlands

Belgium

Berlin

Poland

Slovakia

Hungary

France

Yugoslavia

Switzerland

Austria

Germany 1940

To children everywhere:
May you always find inspirations to feed your imaginations.

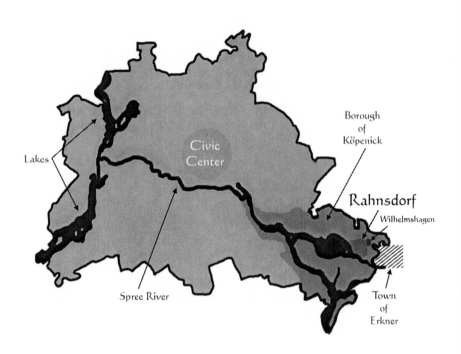

Lakes

Borough
of
Köpenick

Civic
Center

Rahnsdorf

Wilhelmshagen

Spree River

Town
of
Erkner

Berlin

If flowers can grow through wind and rain
and storm, so can we!

Angel Seguin

The difference between stumbling blocks
and stepping stones is how you use them.

Unknown,
in *Woman's World*

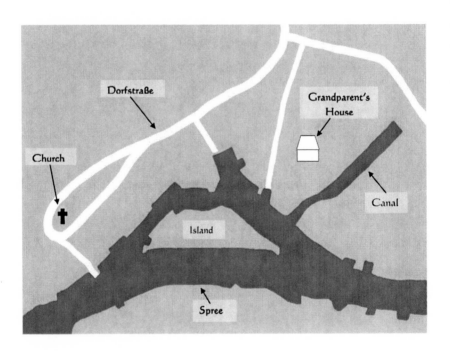

Old-Town Rahnsdorf

Oma's Secret Recipe

CONTENTS

CHAPTERS

SONGS

APPENDICES

Old-Town Rahnsdorf

Vorspeise

*L*ina Bhero was born in 1937 in her maternal grandparents' house in Rahnsdorf; though at that time her parents Henka and Kellman shared a house with Lina's Aunt Bathilda, Uncle Eward and Cousin Holleb in the town of Erkner, a suburb of Berlin. It was not unusual among ethnic Polish people to bring a baby into the world at home with the help of the family matriarch and a midwife. As was the custom, several members of the extended family would take part in raising Lina. Later, during World War II, it became a necessity.

Rahnsdorf is far away from Berlin's busy civic center. It started as a fishing village some eight-hundred years ago where the Spree River flows into Lake Müggelsee. Later the settlement became part of the borough of Köpenick, just inside the southeastern city limit of Berlin.

The house of Lina's grandparents with its large garden was built on a street paved with cobblestones. Lina's *Oma* Zezilia and *Opa* Pietrek also owned several acres of grazing land nearby where they raised chickens, rabbits, goats, geese, and sheep. But by the time Lina and her mother, along with Bathilda and Holleb, moved in after being bombed out in Erkner on March 8, 1944, only one goat, a rabbit, and a few chickens were left. Soon they were gone too. Food was scarce. To supplement the fruits and vegetables growing in the garden, Henka and Bathilda helped their father turn a large area of the grazing land into a potato field by digging up the grass with spades and hoes.

There were no other men around to help them. Kellman and Eward got drafted into the German Army early on. And so did Holleb when he became a teenager. Lina didn't see her father for many years. No wonder that she did not recognize him when he unexpectedly arrived for a visit. Kellman—while being reassigned from the eastern front to Italy—was given permission see if his family had survived the total destruction of Erkner.

By the fall of 1944 it became obvious that Lina would have a little brother or sister shortly after the end of the year. Her mother stopped working in the potato field and began helping around the house where she could closely watch over her daughter. Until then, Lina spent her days mostly in the company of her *Oma*, since she had no playmates and did not attend school at that time.

Rahnsdorf

S-Bahn

Train-Station

Rahnsdorf

Bohnenkraut

I slid down the wobbly, creaking banister backside first and landed with a plop on the tiles in the hallway—a mere foot away from my mother who was about to leave the house. It was a beautiful spring day, and I couldn't wait to go outside after breakfast. There was nothing more fun than exploring *Oma* and *Opa's* urban farm now that we were living there.

Of course, I had visited my grandparents before, but not very often and usually just for a couple of hours in the afternoon. To get there, we took the *S-Bahn* from Erkner to Rahnsdorf and walked about two kilometers from the train station. *Mutti* said that she did not like to walk back after dark because the return trip could be interrupted at any time by an air raid. "It is stressful enough having to run to a bomb shelter during daylight hours," she said.

As I found my footing on the floor, *Mutti* spun around. She grabbed my shoulder with her left hand and shook the banister with her right. "See how rickety this is? You could have fallen off and hurt yourself," she said. Her voice was shaky. The frown on her forehead deepened and her eyes twitched as if she was going to cry. "Don't scare me like this ever again! You hear?"

She pushed me with a gentle shove toward my grandmother who stood at the threshold to the kitchen.

"You will have your hands full with Lina today," she said to *Oma*. "*Ach ja,* she is a real tomboy."

"So were you when you were seven," said *Oma*. "Lina has a lot of time to become a lady. Here, Henka, take this bread for your lunch. Oh, and take an ax and the wheelbarrow, too. Tell your father to dig up one of the old tree stumps at the edge of the field; we are out of firewood."

Mutti hesitated at the door.

"Don't worry about Lina," said *Oma,* "she'll be fine. Go. Your father and Bathilda left an hour ago. They will need your help to finish the tilling before we have another rain storm."

I didn't know what it meant to be a lady. I wondered if my mother was a lady. Or *Oma*. Or Aunt Bathilda. And I wondered if a lady ever had any fun. The grownups I knew were working all the time. Even at home.

As soon as *Mutti* was out of the door, my grandmother took a bristle brush and began sweeping the large cavity of the wood-burning stove in the kitchen. The ashes fell into a wide-mouthed pail which she held in front of the oven door.

The kitchen was very tight. *Oma* with her ample waist could barely move around in it. The space was small even when there were only two chairs at the table. Now there were six, though we only needed five when we were all together in the evening. The extra chair was for my cousin Holleb—in case he should come home from his military training.

Oma's Secret Recipe

My breakfast was already on the table. Eager to get outside and feel the sunshine on my skin, I shoveled the cold, leftover oatmeal from the day before into my mouth as fast as I could. Besides, not wanting to be in *Oma's* way gave me one more reason to get out of the house quickly. In my haste, the last dollop of food fell on the table. I scooped it up and ate it anyway.

"*Oma,* can I go outside now?" I asked, still chewing on a bit of food I had licked from the spoon before leaving it in the blue-enameled bowl.

"*Ja, ja,* you may. But don't wander out onto the street."

As I jumped down from the wooden chair at the kitchen table, I slipped on a bit of oatmeal which I had dropped on the floor. I stumbled and knocked the pail out of my grandmother's hand. Cinder and ashes scattered all over the floor and onto the table and chairs, as well as all over *Oma* and me. We were both coughing and sneezing.

"Well," said *Oma,* "Now you will have to wait to go outside until I have you cleaned up. Take off your clothes. Your shoes and socks, too."

"But I will just get dirty again outside," I protested.

"I don't want you to grind the ashes into the fabric. They are hard enough to get out as it is."

I kicked my shoes under the table and wiggled out of my dress. "Can I go outside now? I like being barefoot."

"*Nein.* Not in your undies."

"But I have to feed the frogs, lizards, and caterpillars."

"They can feed themselves."

"There is nothing for them to eat in the jars where I keep them."

"You must let them go. They belong in the garden," said *Oma*.

"But I have nothing to play with . . . not even a ball," I said, sulking.

"Find something other than those critters. Use your imagination."

She took a damp rag and began wiping my face, neck, arms and legs, as well as one of the chairs. "Sit here while I clean up the rest."

She left the rag on the kitchen table and pulled another piece of scrap fabric out of a basket.

There was nothing for me to do but to sit and watch. I had only two dresses and *Mutti* had placed the other one into the dirty-clothes hamper the night before.

I picked up the spoon and started drumming on the table, and then on the cereal bowl.

"If you keep this up we will both get a headache," said *Oma* without turning around to look at me.

I put the spoon down and let my thoughts wander to all the things I was missing by being confined to the kitchen.

Just for once, though, I was glad that Holleb was not around to see what had happened—even though I missed him very much. He would have surely teased me for the rest of the day. In my mind I could hear him call me Cinderella. And I imagined sticking out my tongue at him and saying, "My name isn't Ella. It's Lina!" But he'd probably laugh and start calling me Cinderlina instead. *Ach!*

With nothing else to do, I picked up the spoon again and began drawing doodles in the ashes that had landed on the table. The circles I made got bigger and bigger until the spoon came in contact with the rag which *Oma* had left at the far end. Using the spoon, I pulled that damp rag toward me. Then, seeing how *Oma* was cleaning the kitchen, I started imitating her back-and-forth motion. And before long I had cleaned the entire tabletop all by myself.

I was quite proud of my accomplishment, especially when *Oma* praised me for my effort.

"I will tell your *Mutti* that you are growing up really fast," she said to me. And then she muttered to herself, "Henka is missing much more than she is realizing."

"Can I help you with something else, *Oma?*"

"*Nein.* I'll have to do the washing and you are not yet big enough to help me with that."

"*Bitte? Bitte? Bitte? Bitte? Bitte?*" I pleaded. The thought of having to sit and watch *Oma* do another repetitive household chore seemed utterly boring. I started fidgeting and then pulled on her apron. I begged and begged until she relented.

Oma let out a sigh. "Seems like I won't get any work done if I don't keep you busy." She lifted me back up on a chair. "Now wait here. I'll be right back." Then she went upstairs.

After a few minutes *Oma* returned with one of *Opa's* better shirts. "You can wear this," she said. "I've been putting it aside in case Holleb comes home, so don't ruin it." She bent down to fold up the sleeves and then tied the shirt tails into a knot. I felt like I was wearing a collapsed tent, but at least I could accompany *Oma* outside.

We walked to the back of the yard and went into the shed that *Opa* had built with his own hands. There were neatly arranged tools hanging from hooks and pegs on one side of the door. On the opposite side were stacks of less-often used items, including *Oma's* washboard. Further back, on shelves, I saw rows of glass jars. Some of them were still filled with vegetables from the previous harvest. I stood transfixed before a jar of green beans when I heard *Oma* say, "You can have those for lunch. But right now, see if you can find an old newspaper or some wood chips to help me light a fire."

There weren't any wood chips, but I did find a couple of pages from an old newspaper which I put near the door. I walked back to the shelves and reached for the green beans.

"Don't touch those jars," said *Oma*, "We don't want to have another accident."

Using a crowbar, she tried to pull off a board from the inside wall of the shed.

"Why are you doing this?" I wanted to know, since I certainly would have been punished for willfully destroying anything.

"I need wood for the stove," she said, huffing. Though *Oma* tried to loosen the board in several places up and down the wall, it didn't budge. She finally gave up when she was completely out of breath.

Returning the crowbar to its place, *Oma* picked up the washboard and placed it under her left arm. Then she took a saw down from a peg to hold in her left hand and, with her right, took a jar of green beans from the shelf.

"Let's go back to the kitchen," she said. "You can open the door for me. And don't forget to bring the newspaper."

That day I learned why the banister was so unstable. My grandmother burned one of the supporting posts when she ran out of firewood.

I also saw how hard *Oma* had to scrub to get the laundry clean on a washboard. It took all morning to wash just one change of clothing for five of us. When all of the shirts, trousers, dresses, and stockings were on the line, my grandmother made lunch. She put the green beans into a pot and added some potatoes. As the stew was simmering on the stove, *Oma* crumpled some dried leaves between her fingers and sprinkled them into the pot.

"What's that?" I wanted to know.

"Savory leaves . . . savory is an herb. You know, like rosemary, parsley and thyme."

That evening I told my mother, "I like *Oma's* green beans the best. She makes them taste good with savory."

"Really?" said *Mutti.* "I always make my green bean with potato stews from the same recipe. I add some savory and the *Mehlschwitze,* too. Except that whenever I could not get any butter, I had to make the *Mehlschwitze* with just flour and water." She looked at her mother. "Did you use butter today?" *Oma* shook her head from side to side. *Mutti* turned back to me and said, "I guess you were extra hungry today."

I knew better than to argue with my mother. She would have sent me to bed early. But I was convinced that the green beans always tasted better when my grandmother made them for me. *Oma* didn't say anything, but I saw a little smile on her face as she was turning away.

Kümmel

ᴺot even the gathering clouds that threatened to open into a deluge could stop *Oma* from doing her daily washing of the work clothes for *Opa, Mutti* and Aunt Bathilda. Field work is very dusty. Besides, they had only one change each, as my mother and her sister had to wear some of their father's clothes. We had left with nothing but what we were wearing when we escaped from the bombing raid that had flattened our house in Erkner. And we had no money to buy new outfits or even used ones.

That summer, playing near the clothes line that *Oma* had extended to stretch from the house half way to the tool shed, I saw *Mutti* coming back from the meadow-turned-potato field where she, her sister and their father were usually working all day. *Mutti* was carrying a large canister. I thought she was returning for drinking water since it wasn't time for supper yet. But *Opa* and Aunt Bathilda also came back. I followed them inside. Suddenly, there was a flash of lightening in the sky, followed, a few seconds later, by deep rumblings of thunder. *Oma* grabbed a basket. *"Mach schnell!"* she said to *Mutti* and Aunt Bathilda. "We have to get the clothes off the line before it starts to rain."

"I'll help," I said, as I followed them outside.

"*Nein,* go back inside," said *Oma.*

"You will only be in the way," added *Mutti.*

Reluctantly, I turned around and collided with *Opa* who was in the hallway putting on his jacket.

"Where are you going?" I asked.

"To do some work in the shed," he said.

"Can I help you?"

"*Nein.*"

"Can I go to your room and look at pictures of spiders in the encyclopedia?"

"We can do that later."

He closed the door behind him and I went back into the kitchen. Looking around for something to do, I spotted a notebook next to several small jars on a shelf. They were high up on the wall, though quite close to the stove. 'Maybe there are pictures in that book' I thought, 'I sure would like to look inside.' Then I remembered that one of the jars contained the dried savory that *Oma* put into all of her green-bean dishes. Since I really like the taste of herbs in my food, the temptation to see what was in those other jars and to get the notebook became irresistible. Though there had been a fire in the stove that morning, it had gone out hours ago. I pulled a chair next to it and climbed on up. Steadying myself with one hand on the stove pipe I reached up with the other. Though I stretched up as high as I could and even got on my toes, the notebook and the jars were out of my reach. I was just about to lose my balance when I heard *Oma* and *Mutti* come back into the house. Thankfully, I managed to jump off the chair without hurting myself.

"Easy there," said **Oma**. She moved the chair back to the table. "Sit here. Or you can help your mother with the folding."

"Where is *Tante* Tilda?"

"She is helping your **Opa**."

Mutti sat down next to me at the table. "We are lucky the neighbors traded us eggs for our firewood. What are you going to do with them?" she asked, as she began folding the laundry.

"*Salzburger Nockerl*," said **Oma**. "Your father told me he had to work extra hard to dig up that old willow-tree stump. The roots are so invasive. I want to surprise him with his favorite dessert." She put some wood chips into the cavity of the stove and lit a few matches, one after another. But each time the tiny flame went out before the wood caught on fire. **Oma** let out a sigh. "The chips are not dry enough," she said. Then she reached up, took the notebook, opened it, tore out a couple of pages, crumpled them up and used them to light a fire.

"These are your recipes," said *Mutti*, looking aghast.

"What good are recipes when you can't get most of the ingredients?" said **Oma**. "Besides, they are only reminders of how much we have lost already and may be deprived of forever."

"Unlike you," said *Mutti*, "I find comfort in remembering recipes; especially for dishes which Kellman cooked for me before he went into the Army."

"And what is he cooking now? Watery barley soup for the soldiers? What a waste of a great chef!"

SALZBURGER NOCKERL

5 egg whites and 3 yolks (separated)
3 tablespoons sugar
2 tablespoons flour
1 teaspoon vanilla
1 pinch salt
Rind of 1 lemon (optional)
powdered sugar (optional)
Sweet butter for greasing a dish
1/4 cup milk

Preheat a medium-sized, buttered baking dish
to which the milk has been added in a hot oven.
Meanwhile, beat the egg yolks together with the
vanilla, grated lemon rind, and the flour.
In a separate dish, beat the egg whites with the
salt. Add the sugar one spoonful at a time
until soft peaks form. Fold the egg yolks into
the egg whites until just blended. Spoon the
mixture into the preheated baking dish and
bake 8 to 10 minutes in the middle of the oven
until lightly browned. Sprinkle with powdered
sugar, if desired, and serve at once.
Enjoy.

"Indeed" said *Mutti*. "But the war has to end sometime. Let's hope that all of us will see better times very soon. I want to pass on our family's recipes to Lina. Let me see your book."

Oma handed it to her.

"Are there any recipes from *Vati* in there?" I wanted to know, remembering how my mother would recite my father's recipes in great detail to pass the time whenever we had to sit out an air raid in a bomb shelter.

Mutti leafed through the notebook. "*Ja*, some of them are. Here is one for goulash." She scanned the page. "Oh," she said, looking intently at *Oma*, "he even told you his secret about adding a pinch of chopped caraway seeds and lemon peel at the end."

The mention of a secret piqued my curiosity, since my mother constantly reminded me not to repeat any family discussions outside of the house. She would say, "Remember, it is very important to keep everything being said in the family a secret. Especially anything that sounds unusual."

"*Mutti*, what is lemon peel?"

"It is the skin from a fruit that we cannot grow here."

"Why not?"

"Because lemon trees don't grow where there is snow and ice in the winter."

"Then where do lemons come from?"

"From Italy."

"Is that the secret?" I wanted to know, just to be sure.

"*Nein*," said *Mutti*. "But leaving out an ingredient from a recipe on purpose is. That is keeping a secret. Your *Vati* once told me that some cooks do that so others can't make food taste as good as they can."

"He must have been talking about professional cooks," said *Oma*. "They can be very competitive."

"*Ja*. Maybe," said *Mutti*. "But what about you? Should I suspect that that's the reason why Lina likes your cooking better than mine?"

"Nonsense, Henka. You are my daughter. The recipes I gave you are exact copies of the ones my mother gave me. Look, you can check them yourself."

"What other recipes are in there *Mutti*?" I asked. "Please read some to me."

She scanned some pages. "Here is one for making *Königsberger Marzipan*."

"My favorite candy. I wish I had some right now."

"*Ach*, Lina, we don't have any almonds."

"Besides, sugary treats will only rot your teeth," said *Oma*.

"That's what *Mutti* always says, too. But she gives me sweets anyway."

"*Ja*," admitted *Mutti*. "And once, when we had nothing else for supper, I gave her a slice of bread sprinkled with a little bit of sugar and a few drops of water to keep the sugar from falling off." She handed the notebook to her mother, who put it back on the shelf.

KÖNIGSBERGER MARZIPAN

1/2 kg sweet almonds
15 grams bitter almonds
1/2 kg powdered sugar
Rose water

Blanch the almonds, let them cool, and peel. Grate the almonds very fine and combine them with sugar and rose water to form dough. When the dough is pliable without sticking to your hands, roll it out on a sugar-sprinkled surface to the width of your thumb. Then cut the dough into bars or use cookie cutters to cut out shapes. Place the candies on a baking sheet. Bake in a lukewarm oven until firm, but not dry.
Enjoy.

When *Mutti* was finished folding the laundry, she took the basket full of clothes upstairs.

"While you are up there, see if you can find something we can spare to unravel," *Oma* called after her. "Lina's socks need darning."

Mutti returned with a faded brown scarf. "This looks like something we can spare, but it may be too felted to unravel. I also found a blue sweater with moth holes in it. If you let me use that, then we'll have plenty of yarn to mend socks and even knit some new ones."

"*Ja, ja.* Go get it and find the knitting needles, too."

"I will bring them down after I am finished cleaning our bedroom," said *Mutti*. "I should be done by the time dinner is ready."

"*Gut*," said *Oma*. "Lina, stay here with me in the kitchen."

I would have rather gone outside. But meanwhile it had started to rain and it was getting dark.

"*Oma*, what do you keep in those jars up there?" I asked, pointing to the shelf.

"Dried herbs . . . I still have some rosemary, a little savory and some marjoram. But most of them are empty now."

"I hope you don't run out of savory for the green beans."

Oma chuckled. "Don't worry. We can pick fresh herbs now in my kitchen garden. The savory, lovage and dill plants are getting really big. I will start drying some of them soon for next winter. So, I won't even have to improvise."

"Improvise?"

"It means making do with what I have on hand. Once, when I ran out of savory, I used marjoram instead."

"Can you improvise when making *Marzipan?*"

"*Nein.* We don't have any nuts at all." *Oma* stepped into the tiny alcove opposite the kitchen door which she called her pantry. "*Ach* . . . I don't even have enough sugar to make the *Nockerl* . . . and we are out of butter."

"What are you going to do?"

"I guess I will have to improvise much sooner than I thought necessary."

"How?"

"Hmm . . . I can grease a dish with some chicken fat. And there is a little bit of cheese left to sprinkle on top. So, instead of the sweet *Nockerl* I will make a savory soufflé. As long as it is fluffy, your *Opa* will like it."

After beating the egg whites until stiff and combining them with the other ingredients, *Oma* poured the mixture into a baking dish. Using a spoon, she carefully scraped off every last bit of the batter from the whisk and the mixing bowl. There was nothing left on either of them for me to have even one little lick.

"Is this only for *Opa?*" I asked, seeing that the baking dish was just three quarters full.

"It will rise in the oven like a cake," said *Oma.* "We will all get to eat some of it."

She used a spatula to smooth the surface of the batter and

sprinkled the grated cheese on top. "There," she said, "Just enough to give it a little flavor."

Then she opened the oven door and placed the baking dish on the middle rack.

"What else are we going to have?"

"Cabbage soup," she said, as she put the cast-iron pot on the stove which contained the soup she had made the previous day. To conserve fuel, she always made enough soup to last several days.

The rain was coming down hard now and began drumming against the window. While *Oma* was setting the table, she stirred the soup to keep it from burning on the bottom. When steam began to rattle the lid, she took the pot off the stove and set it on a trivet in the middle of the table.

"Now, don't touch this, Lina. It is very hot!" she said, as she stepped into the hallway. *Oma* pulled two umbrellas out of a tall urn. "I am going to tell Pietrek and Bathilda that dinner is ready. You go get your mother."

I knew that it would take several minutes for *Oma, Opa* and my aunt to return. And, instead of going upstairs, I could just call for *Mutti* to come down. So, there was enough time to satisfy my curiosity to see if the soufflé in the oven was increasing in volume as *Oma* had said it would.

I put on a pair of oven mitts and, using both hands, I yanked on the handle until the heavy door sprang open. A hot cloud of steam hit my face. The soufflé—which I saw had risen above the rim as high as the width of three of my fingers—suddenly collapsed. It fell way down into the dish. Startled, I slammed the oven door shut and ran upstairs.

Oma returned before I had a chance to tell my mother that supper was ready. *"Ach du lieber,"* I heard her exclaim. *Mutti* ran down to see what had happened, as I reluctantly followed her into the kitchen.

"What's wrong, mother?" She asked.

"I don't know," said *Oma.* "For some reason, the soufflé did not rise."

"Maybe the stove wasn't hot enough?"

Oma shook her head and said, "The oven is very hot." She looked sad as she pulled the dish out of the oven and put it on top of the stove. *Mutti* handed her a spatula.

"Look at this," said *Oma.* "It doesn't even have the texture of a pancake. I could have saved myself a lot of work if I had just hard-boiled those eggs."

I peeked out from behind my mother, pulling myself up on her dress to have a better look. My cheeks were burning. *Mutti* turned around and said, "Lina, why are you blushing?"

Before I could stammer an answer, *Oma* asked: "Lina, did you open the oven door?"

I just nodded and looked down at the floor. I don't know what felt worse: anticipating punishment or the shame I felt for having caused my grandmother to be so disappointed.

Mutti pushed me away from the stove. "We will talk about this later," she said. "Right now I wonder what we can do with what is left in the dish, *ja.*"

"There is not much we can do with it," said *Oma.* "I will just cut it into little pieces and use it to garnish the soup."

When my grandfather and aunt had joined us at the table, *Mutti* ladled soup into each of our bowls and *Oma* sprinkled a spoonful of chopped-up eggs on top.

"I am glad that we have some protein with the cabbage soup," said Aunt Bathilda, "But this is an unusual combination."

"Couldn't you have done something else with those eggs?" asked *Opa*.

"I was going to surprise you with *Salzburger Nockerl*," said *Oma*, "But when I saw that I did not have enough sugar, I tried to make a cheese-flavored soufflé instead. This is the unfortunate result—after Lina tried to help."

"She opened the oven door before the soufflé was done," said *Mutti*.

Aunt Bathilda looked at me. "Haste makes waste."

"Not entirely," said *Opa*, "At least, it's nourishing."

"It makes a new recipe," I said, feeling somewhat relieved.

Mutti looked at me sternly. "Children should be seen and not heard!" she said, while she scooped up a piece of egg. After chewing on it for a bit, she remarked, "This has a rather odd taste."

"I had to improvise," said *Oma*. "Since we are completely out of butter, I greased the soufflé dish with chicken fat."

"It tastes really good," I said, "Like everything that *Oma* makes."

"Hush!" said *Mutti*. "That is not the way to make up for what you did."

I finished my soup in silence, though I knew that I was right about the taste.

"Up to bed with you," said *Mutti*, as soon as I put my spoon down.

I got up from the table, said *"Gute Nacht"* to everyone and slowly climbed up the stairs.

"What am I going to do with this child?" I heard my mother say. "I would like to ground her until she is twenty, *ja*."

"You cannot keep a tomboy grounded for long," said *Oma*. "There is nothing for her to do in your bedroom. She'll go stir crazy. And I can't have her underfoot in the kitchen all the time. We've had too many close calls."

"She can't stay in the living room, either," said Aunt Bathilda. "That's my and Holleb's room now."

"Let's hope the weather will be better tomorrow, so Lina can play outside," said *Opa*. And on that they all agreed.

APFELMUS

Tart or sweet apples
Sugar to taste
Cinnamom or vanilla to taste
White wine (optional)

Peal the apples and cut them into quarters. After removing the cores, rinse the apple pieces before placing them into an enameled pot with a cup of wine or water. Sprinkle the sugar and spices on top and cook on low to medium heat without stirring until the apple pieces fall apart. Strain through a nonmetallic sieve to remove any lumps. Cool before serving. Enjoy.

Liebstöckel

After the fiasco with the soufflé—*Oma's* failed plan to serve a special dinner treat and the shame I felt for having been the cause of it—I tried to help out as much as I could. Though, in retrospect, I didn't try hard enough. So it was no wonder that I was told to play outside whenever the weather was fair. That meant just about all the time.

Thankfully, as the summer went on, *Oma* spent more time out of doors too. Together, we tended her kitchen garden. That's where she grew strawberries, radishes and herbs. It was a narrow strip of land on the side of the house. The main vegetable garden with fruit trees and a hedge of gooseberry bushes was in back. I helped with watering, weeding and pest control—collecting snails. I learned many useful things—like that some weeds are edible. *Oma* used dandelion greens when there was no spinach and added sorrel to soups, salads and sauces.

When the rosemary, thyme and dill got big enough to start flowering, she cut off the stalks and tied the bundles with twine. Then we carried the herb bundles into the shed at the far end of the garden where she hung them upside down on pegs to dry.

Not all herbs were preserved using the drying method. Tender ones would have lost all of their taste. To preserve the flavor of fresh flat-leaf parsley, for example, *Oma* would chop up copious amounts, mix them with a lot of salt, and pack them tightly into jars. So I am told. I didn't get to see the process because I wasn't allowed in the kitchen with all of that knife work going on.

Oma did all sorts of wonderful things with food that my mother never did, and I was determined to learn all of her secrets. For that, I had to find a way to be by her side in the kitchen. Alas, I realized that there was only one way to do it. I had to control my urge to be always in motion. But sitting still with nothing to do was very hard for me. At the very least, I needed to keep my hands busy. Then, one evening I found a way.

All five of us were in the kitchen. The radio was playing.

Looking up from her knitting project, Aunt Bathilda said, "I am sick and tired of hearing these propaganda broadcasts."

Mutti, who was mending my dress, gave her a stern look and said, "Lina is present."

"Sorry," said Aunt Bathilda. "It is hard to control my feelings all the time."

"Lina," said *Opa,* "See if you can find some music instead of the news."

He was whittling a *Quirl* for *Oma* from the top of last-year's Christmas tree to replace the store-bought hand blender which I had broken trying to dig up earthworms in the garden. *Opa* never threw anything away that might come in handy some day.

I walked over to the sideboard and started turning the dial on the radio. All I got was high-pitched whistling and the sound of static.

"Turn it off," said *Opa*. "There is already too much din in this kitchen."

Oma, who was noisily scrubbing pots and washing dishes, just shook her head.

I walked over to my aunt. "What are you knitting, *Tante* Tilda?"

"A scarf for Holleb," she said. "He always catches colds so easily."

"That's pretty." I said. "He likes blue."

"It will be nice and warm. There is enough wool here to knit one for you, too."

"Is knitting hard to do?"

"Not really—as long as it is something simple like a scarf."

"Can you teach me to knit a scarf?"

"I might," she said, looking at *Mutti*. "But you could hurt yourself with a knitting needle. Anyway, we don't have an extra pair."

"I can carve a thicker pair with blunt points for her," said *Opa*.

"*Ja*," said *Mutti*. "She needs something to keep her busy."

"*Danke*," I beamed and went around the kitchen to give each of them a big hug.

The next couple of evenings, Aunt Bathilda taught me how to

knit and pearl. And because I was able to sit still while doing it, I was allowed to spend more time again in the kitchen with *Oma*. That is, until the fall. That's when my mother's stomach got bigger and she began helping around the house. With the canning season approaching and with all the other chores that always needed to be done around the house, my grandmother certainly could use her help. But now I was in the way once more.

"Go outside and play," said *Mutti* when she saw me in the kitchen. "Enjoy being a child."

"But I want to stay in here and knit a little longer," I pleaded.

"*Nein*. It's a sunny day. You can take your knitting outside."

Reluctantly, I left the kitchen. But without my half-finished scarf. To me, knitting was not an outdoor activity.

Wondering what to do next, I started thinking about my cousin Holleb. It would have been fun to have him at home. We hadn't seen him since he went away for his mandatory military training. Though six years older than I was, Holleb taught me many games. One weekend, when we were still living in Erkner, we built a tepee in the back yard. He showed me how to make a bow and arrows and then we took turns playing *"Trapper und Indianer."*

I went to the chicken coop to look for feathers, hoping that there would be enough of them to make a headdress. That had always been my favorite part of our costumes. The chickens were long gone. But since there was no urgent need to clean the space, there were still plenty of feathers strewn about on the ground. I picked one up and saw that it wasn't a brown feather. It was just dirty. Then I saw that even the ones that seemed to be fairly clean were quite grungy-looking when I turned them over. I threw the feathers back on the ground and walked to the water pump to wash my hand. Try as I might, though, I was not strong enough to operate the handle. I had to go to the house to clean myself up.

As I walked back through the garden under the fruit trees, a green apple fell to the ground. It was the first one of the season. I picked it up and smelled it. The aroma made my mouth water and I took a bite. It was not sweet, yet tasted very refreshing. With a finger, I stopped the juice from running down my chin and stuck out my tongue to lick it. I looked up to see if I could pick another one, but all of the apples were too high up. Of course, that was not a deterrent to me. I climbed up the tree and ate one apple after another until my stomach began to ache.

I was sick for the rest of the afternoon and was sent off to bed when I refused to eat dinner. At least I was spared from having to endure another one of my mother's lectures about my wayward ways.

I tossed and turned all night long and still did not feel like eating in the morning. It didn't help that it was my mother's turn to do the cooking.

"Where is *Oma?*" I asked.

"She is picking apples. We are going to make *Apfelmus.*"

"I am not hungry," I said.

"Try to eat anyway. Be thankful that we still have food." She dished out some oatmeal and handed me a spoon.

I scooped up less than half of a spoonful, put it into my mouth and took my time before swallowing.

"Why aren't you eating? Is it not good?"

"I am just not very hungry."

"I know that you prefer your grandmother's cooking."

"This oatmeal tastes the same as always," I said, truthfully. "I don't even mind that it is not very sweet."

I was glad to see that my mother's face became more relaxed. She took the bowl from me and ate my breakfast. "Don't run around on an empty stomach," she said to me, "or you will feel sick again, *ja*."

I sat quietly with my knitting when *Oma* came in from the garden carrying a basket full of apples, which she emptied into the sink.

"Good crop this year," she said. "Looks like we will be using more jars than we have seals for." *Oma* sat down at the table to rest. "Henka," she continued, "Go see if you can buy at least two dozen rubber rings."

"The store here, *im Dorf*?"

"*Nein*. That one does not have any left. Nor do the other stores in Rahnsdorf. Try the ones in Wilhelmshagen. And take your time." *Oma* gave her some money.

After my mother was gone, I accompanied *Oma* into the garden. She took a long-handled tool with a hook at one end and used it to shake apples off the tree. I helped to pick them up. Before I knew, it was time for our mid-day meal.

"I hear you didn't have any breakfast this morning," she said. "Do you think you will be able to eat some noodle soup?"

"*Ja*. That's my favorite—besides string beans."

"*Gut*. Come help me pick some lovage."

When *Mutti* returned with a bagful of rubber rings, I ran up to her and gave her a hug. "I see you are feeling better," she said.

"You were gone sooo long. *Oma* made the best lunch."

"*Ja*? What?" said my mother.

"*Oma* made chicken-noodle soup."

"We don't have any chicken," said my mother. "But I am glad you ate something."

"It tasted just like chicken-noodle soup," I insisted.

Mutti didn't look too pleased. "Did you see any meat in your soup?"

I shook my head. *Mutti* rolled her eyes and looked at *Oma*.

"I made a mock version with lovage," said my grandmother. "I saved some for you. Let me just heat it up."

Mutti washed her hands and sat down next to me. *Oma* handed her a steaming bowl of soup with plenty of noodles, chunks of celery root and carrots, and wilted lovage leaves. "Thankfully, we still have salt," she said, "But it would have been better if we had had some bouillon cubes."

"Lina liked it anyway. She likes whatever you cook," said *Mutti*. She picked up a spoonful and looked at it. Then she looked into the bowl. "What is this greasy film I see on top?"

"Chicken fat," said *Oma*.

"Chicken fat? I thought you had used the last of it months ago, when you tried to make a soufflé." She swished the soup around in her mouth before swallowing. "No wonder Lina thinks that you made chicken noodle soup. Where did you get it?"

"I still have a couple of jars. *Eiserne Ration.*"

"Then why are you using your last reserves now?"

"I have been adding chicken fat to Lina's meals all along—except to oatmeal, of course."

"*Ach,* that is your secret! No wonder Lina likes your cooking so much."

"Don't excite yourself, Henka. I did not do it to show you up. It's just that Lina is so thin. Just skin and bones. She needs it."

"Sorry. I am really grateful that you take care of her whenever I cannot," said *Mutti.* "But why start giving it to me?"

"Because you need the extra nourishment in your condition," said *Oma.*

"What condition?" I wanted to know.

"I told you," said *Mutti.* "You are going to have a little brother or sister next year."

I just nodded.

"You don't look very happy about it," said *Oma.* "Don't you want to have someone to play with?"

Mutti gave me a hug, which brightened my mood immediately. I was so worried that once the baby arrived my mother would no longer have any time for me. I failed to consider a bright side to having a sibling.

"There, that's better," said *Oma.* "I like to see a smile on your face."

Oma's Secret Recipe

When *Mutti* finished eating, the three of us went into the garden to bring more apples inside. We had already made several trips when Aunt Bathilda came from the field to get drinking water for herself and *Opa*.

Oma wiped her brow. "We can all use a rest," she said. "Let's go inside."

"I miss having coffee and cake in the afternoon," said my aunt.

"Be thankful that we can still brew herbal tea," said *Oma*.

Mutti put a kettle with water on the stove and set the table, while Aunt Bathilda went to the pantry to get the *Lindenblütentee* and a tea cozy. While the tea was steeping, we all got cleaned up. *Oma* poured the tea and said, "We are out of sugar, but at least we can always pick more *Lindenblüten*."

"Let's hope that the tree across the street survives the next winter and the war," said *Mutti*.

Oma nodded in agreement. Aunt Bathilda put her cup down and looked at me. "Lina, you are very quiet. And you aren't fidgeting at all."

"Lina has learned that she must control herself if she wants to be in the kitchen . . . especially when I am cooking," said *Oma*.

"She is still a tomboy," said *Mutti*, "but I must admit that her behavior has been improving over the summer."

Aunt Bathilda smiled and said to me. "So, your *Oma* is turning you into a lady."

I blushed.

"*Ja*, that's one recipe I certainly would like to have," said *Mutti* looking at my grandmother. "Why don't you add it to the ones in your notebook?"

"You can call it 'Tomboy Tamer,'" I piped up.

"Hush," said *Mutti*. "Mind your manners. Interrupting is not lady-like behavior." She took a sip of tea before continuing her lecture. "You still have a long way to go. And be thankful. You are very lucky that there is always someone to look after you whenever I cannot."

"I know," I said, feeling quite contrite. "Aunt Bathilda has always watched over me when we were living in Erkner. And now, here in Rahnsdorf, *Oma* does too.

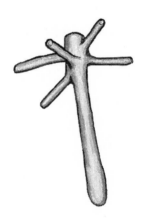

Lindenblüten

Pietrek (Opa and Oma) **Zezilia**

Nachspeise

ꞌWhat were Lina's experiences in the suburb of Erkner before she moved in with her grandparents in Berlin-Rahnsdorf? Why wasn't her mother taking care of her all of the time? What else did her aunt Bathilda do? How did Lina survive the bombing of Erkner on March 8, 1944? Did she ever see her cousin Holleb again? Was she ever as close to her grandfather as she was to her grandmother? How did she react when the soldier who entered her grandparent's house unannounced turned out to be her father? Why was it so important to be secretive? And what happened to Lina and her family after 1944? These and many other questions are answered in *My Berlin: Childhood Reflections*, a collection of stories and songs that take the reader to the end of the war.

Future editions for this series include *My Berlin: A Teenager's Life*, in which Lina Bhero reflects on living in East-Berlin after 1948; and *My Berlin: A Lasting Legacy*, in which she reveals how her experiences as a youth in Berlin continue to influence her life in the United States.

Bathilda
(Tante Tilda)

Henka
(Mutti)

My Berlin

YOU LEFT ME A LEGACY

By CHRISTEL ALEXANDER
and TODD SCHROEDER

My Berlin

YOU DESERVED MUCH MORE

By CHRISTEL ALEXANDER
and TODD SCHROEDER

Oma's Secret Recipe

Instrumental Solo

My Berlin

Garden

My Berlin

SPIDER ON MY WINDOW SCREEN

Lyrics and Music by
CHRISTEL ALEXANDER

Oma's Secret Recipe

My Berlin

This watch-ful spi-der's al-ways on her guard,
catch-ing prey that could well prey on me.
Till the day my moth-er razed her net;
Mak-ing sure the win-dow looks clean.
Now there're flies a-plen-ty fear-ing no threat from
spi-ders on my win-dow screen.
I miss see-ing my friend Jean, the
Spi-der On My Win-dow Screen.

Rahnsdorf

Train-Station
Erkner

Train-Station
Rahnsdorf

GLOSSARY
of
German Terms

(Note: German nouns and cognates are capitalized in the text to facilitate recognition.)

Ach du lieber . . . . Oh, my goodness

Ach . . . . Alas / so

Apfelmus . . . . Applesauce

Bitte . . . . Please

Bohnenkraut . . . . Savory

Danke (pronounced DAHÑke) . . . . Thank you

Eiserne Ration . . . . Emergency rations / last reserves

Im Dorf . . . . In old town

Gut (pronounced GOOT) . . . . Good / okay

Gute Nacht . . . . Good night

Ja (pronounced JAH) . . . . Yes / indeed / just / surely / for sure

Kindergarten . . . . Preschool / after-school activities facility

Königsberger Marzipan . . . . Candy made from almond paste

Kümmel . . . . Caraway / caraway seed(s)

Liebstöckel . . . . Lovage

Lindenblüten . . . . The blossoms of the linden tree

Lindenblütentee . . . Tea made from dried blossoms of a linden tree

Mach schnell . . . . Hurry up

Mehlschwitze . . . . Roux

Mutti (pronounced MOOTtee) . . . . Mom, mama

Nachspeise . . . . Last course / meal ender

Nein (pronounced NINE) . . . . No

Salzburger Nockerl . . . . A sweet dessert soufflé a la Saltzburg

Oma (pronounced OHmah) . . . . Grandma

Opa (pronounced OHpah) . . . . Grandpa

Quirl . . . . A kitchen tool used for blending

S-Bahn . . . . City and suburban train

Tante (pronounced TAHNte) . . . . Aunt

Trapper und Indianer . . . . . Trapper and Native-American Indian

Vati (pronounced FAHtee) . . . . Dad, papa

Vorspeise . . . . First Course / meal starter

ACKNOWLEDGMENTS

Foremost, I like to thank Todd Schroeder. Without his input, this book would not have come into being. I am most grateful for his suggestions, comments, critique, and editing of the text; for arranging and recording the songs, and for his friendship, patience, and kindness. I am also indebted to Mark Winkler for helping me to explore my life experiences as an inspiration for writing lyrics, and to Phil Swann for showing me how to go outside of my comfort zone in writing music.

I like to thank Keri Kelsey for her positive feedback and ever enthusiastic support, who, with Todd Schroeder, leads *The Complete Cabaret Workshop* at Tom Rolla's Gardenia Supper Club in Hollywood, CA; and to Elliot Zwiebach, whose show review of *This Was My Berlin* in *Cabaret Scenes* encouraged me to keep on expanding my stories and songs on this theme.

Also of immense help were the members of the Write Away group in Santa Monica, California, who listened as I told them my stories at the beginning of the writing process. As the work progressed, I built on questions posed by Monona Wali, and also incorporated valuable suggestions received from Judy Marasco. I am very grateful to all of you, as well as to my receptive audience.

Rahnsdorf

Erkner

Berlin

CPSIA information can be obtained
at www.ICGtesting.com
Printed in the USA
LVOW08s1309150517
534576LV00001B/103/P